Chinese New Year
wishes

zhōng guó xīn nián zhù fú
中国新年祝福

JILLIAN LIN

Illustrations by SHI MENG

Hi! I am Hong.

This is my favorite time of the year.

My whole family celebrates.

It is Chinese New Year.

你 好，我 是 虹。

这 是 我 一 年 中 最 喜 欢 的 时 候。

我 全 家 人 都 在 庆 祝。

这 是 中 国 的 新 年。

The house has to be spotless.

We clean it from top to bottom.

I hang up red and gold decorations.

It will give us good luck next year.

<ruby>屋<rt>wū</rt></ruby><ruby>里<rt>lǐ</rt></ruby><ruby>必<rt>bì</rt></ruby><ruby>须<rt>xū</rt></ruby><ruby>一<rt>yì</rt></ruby><ruby>尘<rt>chén</rt></ruby><ruby>不<rt>bù</rt></ruby><ruby>染<rt>rǎn</rt></ruby>。

<ruby>我<rt>wǒ</rt></ruby><ruby>们<rt>men</rt></ruby><ruby>上<rt>shàng</rt></ruby><ruby>上<rt>shàng</rt></ruby><ruby>下<rt>xià</rt></ruby><ruby>下<rt>xià</rt></ruby><ruby>打<rt>dǎ</rt></ruby><ruby>扫<rt>sǎo</rt></ruby><ruby>干<rt>gān</rt></ruby><ruby>净<rt>jìng</rt></ruby>。

<ruby>我<rt>wǒ</rt></ruby><ruby>挂<rt>guà</rt></ruby><ruby>上<rt>shàng</rt></ruby><ruby>红<rt>hóng</rt></ruby><ruby>色<rt>sè</rt></ruby><ruby>和<rt>hé</rt></ruby><ruby>金<rt>jīn</rt></ruby><ruby>色<rt>sè</rt></ruby><ruby>的<rt>de</rt></ruby><ruby>饰<rt>shì</rt></ruby><ruby>物<rt>wù</rt></ruby>。

<ruby>这<rt>zhè</rt></ruby><ruby>会<rt>huì</rt></ruby><ruby>给<rt>gěi</rt></ruby><ruby>我<rt>wǒ</rt></ruby><ruby>们<rt>men</rt></ruby><ruby>明<rt>míng</rt></ruby><ruby>年<rt>nián</rt></ruby><ruby>带<rt>dài</rt></ruby><ruby>来<rt>lái</rt></ruby><ruby>好<rt>hǎo</rt></ruby><ruby>运<rt>yùn</rt></ruby>。

Grandpa takes me to the temple.

We pray for peace and happiness.

I shake a box of bamboo sticks.

It tells me I will be lucky next year!

爷爷带我去寺庙。

我们祈求和平与快乐。

我求竹签。

竹签说我明年会走好运。

Tomorrow is Chinese New Year.

Our family gets together for dinner.

The table is full of yummy food.

I love the noodles and dumplings!

míng tiān shì zhōng guó nóng lì xīn nián
明 天 是 中 国 农 历 新 年。

wǒ men quán jiā yì qǐ chī nián yè fàn
我 们 全 家 一 起 吃 年 夜 饭。

mǎn zhuō dōu shì měi wèi de shí wù
满 桌 都 是 美 味 的 食 物。

wǒ xǐ huān chī miàn tiáo hé jiǎo zi
我 喜 欢 吃 面 条 和 饺 子!

It is the first day of the New Year.

I wear new clothes and shoes.

My parents give me a red packet.

With the money I can buy a toy car!

今天是大年初一。

我穿新衣服和新鞋。

我父母给我一个红包。

我可以用来买一辆玩具车！

We watch the New Year's parade.

A huge red dragon is dancing.

The booming drums make lots of noise.

Happy Chinese New Year!

wǒ men kàn xīn nián yóu xíng
我 们 看 新 年 游 行。

yǒu wǔ lóng shì yì tiáo hěn dà de hóng lóng
有 舞 龙，是 一 条 很 大 的 红 龙。

gǔ qiāo dé hěn xiǎng
鼓 敲 得 很 响。

xīn nián kuài lè
新 年 快 乐！

结束 **The End** jié sù

The Story of Chinese New Year

zhōng guó xīn nián de gù shì
中国新年的故事

Long ago lived a monster called Nian.

He stayed on a mountain.

Each winter, he got hungry.

He ran down to steal people's food.

hěn jiǔ yǐ qián yǒu yí gè guài shòu jiào nián
很 久 以 前 有 一 个 怪 兽, 叫 年。

tā zhù zài shān shàng
他 住 在 山 上。

měi gè dōng tiān tā dū huì è
每 个 冬 天 他 都 会 饿。

tā huì pǎo xià shān qù tōu rén men de shí wù
他 会 跑 下 山 去 偷 人 们 的 食 物。

People were scared of the monster.

They hid away in their houses.

One day, an old man came.

'I am not afraid of Nian,' he said.

rén men hěn hài pà zhè gè guài shòu
人 们 很 害 怕 这 个 怪 兽。

tā men cáng zài wū lǐ
他 们 藏 在 屋 里。

yǒu yī tiān lái le yí wèi lǎo rén
有 一 天，来 了 一 位 老 人。

tā shuō wǒ bù pà nián
他 说："我 不 怕 年。"

He stuck red paper on doors.

He lit lanterns everywhere.

He made loud noises.

'Copy what I do,' he said.

他 在 门 上 都 贴 了 红 纸。

他 到 处 点 亮 灯 笼。

他 做 出 很 大 的 噪 音。

他 说:"跟 我 一 样 做。"

Nian came and heard the noises.

'Help!' he screamed and ran away.

Each new year, people did the same.

And no one has seen Nian ever since.

nián lái de shí hòu tīng dào zhè xiē zào yīn
年 来 的 时 候 听 到 这 些 噪 音。

jiù mìng tā jiān jiào zhe pǎo kāi le
"救 命！" 他 尖 叫 着 跑 开 了。

měi gè xīn nián rén men dōu zhè yàng zuò
每 个 新 年，人 们 都 这 样 做。

cóng nà yǐ hòu zài méi yǒu rén jiàn guò nián
从 那 以 后 再 没 有 人 见 过 年。

结束 The End jié sù

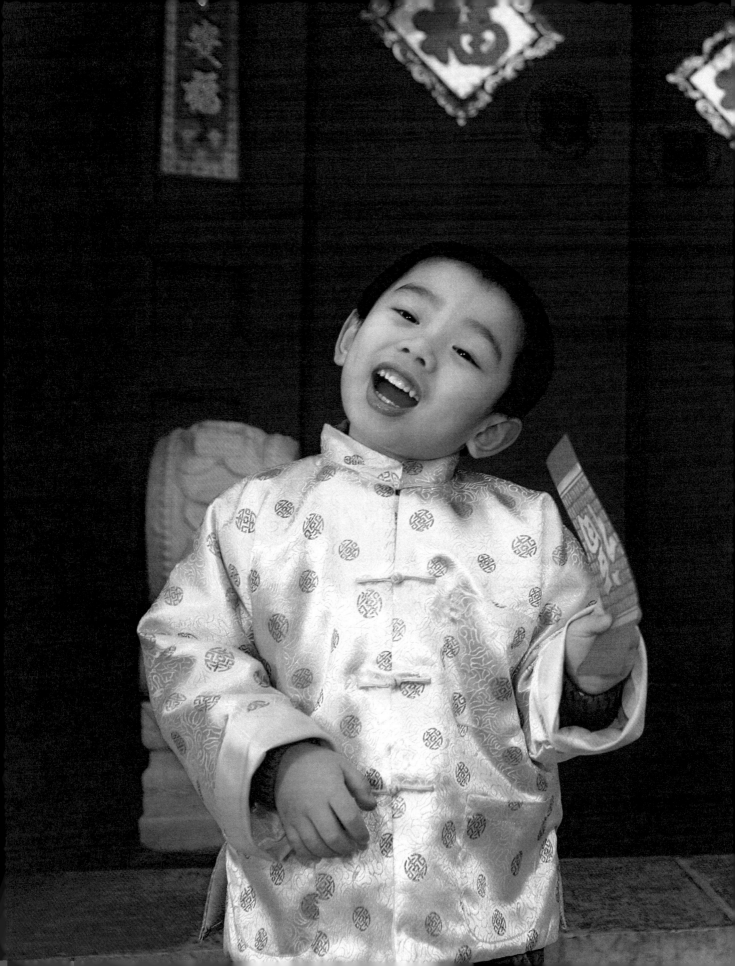

To wish someone 'Happy Chinese New Year' in Chinese, you say *'Shin nyen kwai le'* or *'Gong shee fa tsai'*. A red packet is *'hong bao'*.

新 年 快 乐 !
Xīnnián kuàilè!
Happy new year!

恭 喜 发 财!
Gōngxǐ fācái!
Wishing you success!

红 包
hóngbāo
red packet

23

The Chinese New Year holiday is a busy time. Altogether, people in China take three billion trips by bus, train and air to visit their families. In which holiday does your family get together? What do you do?

春节假期是很忙的，人们乘坐汽车，火车和飞机去旅行或探亲，高达三十亿人次。你的家人在哪个假期聚在一起？你们又做什么？

2020 | 2032
2019 | 2031
2018 | 2030
2021 | 2033
2017 | 2029
2010 | 2022
2011 | 2023
2016 | 2028
2012 | 2024
2015 | 2027
2013 | 2025
2014 | 2026

Each Chinese year is named after one of 12 animals: the rat, ox, tiger, rabbit, dragon, snake, horse, goat, monkey, rooster, dog, and pig.
In which year were you born?
Which animal are you?

zhōng guó nóng lì yǒu shēng xiào měi nián dōu yǐ
中 国 农 历 有 12 生 肖，每 年 都 以
qí zhōng yí gè wéi míng tā men shì shǔ
其 中 一 个 为 名。他 们 是：鼠，
niú hǔ tù lóng shé mǎ yáng hóu
牛，虎，兔，龙，蛇，马，羊，猴，
jī gǒu hé zhū nǐ shì nǎ nián shēng de
鸡，狗 和 猪。你 是 哪 年 生 的？
nǐ de shēng xiào shì shén me
你 的 生 肖 是 什 么？

The last day of the New Year is called the Lantern Festival. Children carry lanterns and solve riddles.

Riddle: what belongs to you, but others use it more than you do?

xīn nián de zuì hòu yì tiān bèi chēng wèi yuán xiāo jié.
新年的最后一天被称为元宵节。
hái zi men dài zhe dēng lóng jiě dēng mí
孩子们带着灯笼，解灯谜。

mí yǔ yǒu shén me shì shǔ yú nǐ de dàn qí tā
谜语：有什么是属于你的，但其他
rén bǐ nǐ yòng dé gèng duō
人比你用得更多？

Other books by Jillian Lin

Moon Festival Wishes
Dragon Boat Festival Wishes
(3–6 years)
English–中文

Find out how families prepare for and celebrate the Moon (or Mid-autumn) and Dragon Boat festivals. Children will also also enjoy reading the stories behind these two important Chinese celebrations.

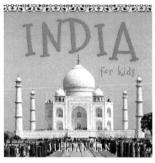 

The *Asia For Kids* series
(3-6 years)

Fun facts and colourful photographs take children on a journey to various countries in Asia and help them discover different cultures.

 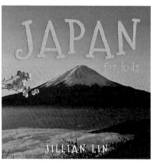 

Also available as e-books on Amazon.
For more information and to get a free e-book, visit
www.jillianlin.com

'A fun way for children to find out about the history of China'

China has a long history, but its many stories are often too complex for children. Jillian Lin has retold these tales so they are easy and fun to read. Children get a glimpse inside the lives of famous Chinese figures including the philosopher Confucius, the first emperor of The Great Wall, and the doctor who invented anaesthetics.

The *Heroes Of China* series (2-6 years) English–中文

The *Once Upon A Time In China...* series (6-12 years)

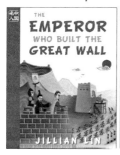  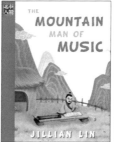 

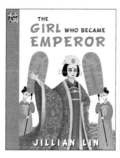   

I hope you enjoyed reading this book. If so, I'd be over the moon if you could leave a review!

Chinese New Year Wishes

Made in United States
North Haven, CT
21 November 2024

60738887R00020